Fatherless Woman

Poems by June Beisch

CAPE COD LITERARY PRESS

Thanks to the Virginia Center for the Arts for the residence that afforded me the time, space and privacy (and a grand piano) necessary for completion of some of these poems.

My heartfelt gratitude to Gillian Drake and the Cape Cod Literary Trust for their support and encouragement and for making this book possible. Thanks also to David Dodd Lee, Barbara Helfgott Hyett, Susan Donnelly and Anne Garton. Thanks also to friends far and near who read these poems with interest, and to my family, especially Chuck, Brooks and Leigh.

© June Beisch, 2004

PUBLISHED BY

Cape Cod Literary Press

P. O. Box 720, North Eastham, MA 02651

(508) 255-5084

ISBN: 1-888959-75-4

PRINTED IN THE UNITED STATES OF AMERICA

ACKNOWLEDGMENTS

Grateful acknowledgment is made to the editors of the following journals in which some of these poems were first published:

The Harvard Review: "The Great Bird Books"

The Radcliffe Quarterly: "Poem for Midlife"

A Sense of Place Anthololgy: "Insomnia,"
                                    "Adding some words to my mother's gravestone"
                                    "Amaryllis"
                                    "Notes from a poetry workshop"

CapeWomen Magazine: "Selling the House"
                                    "Nauset Beach"
                                    "Amaryllis"
                                    "Notes from a poetry workshop"

The Literary Review: "Continental Drift"

The Florida Review: "Kale Soup"

Tendril Magazine: "Fatherless Woman"

Northeast Corridor: "Professor of Apocalypse"

The Paterson Literary Review: "Driving to the Cape"

Epiphany Magazine: "The Painters"

North Essex Review: "The Keats House"

Pebble Lake Review: "Love"

Bodies of Land: "Venice," "Leaving Concord,"
                                    "The Amtrack Poem"

Some of these poems appeared in a chapbook, *Take Notes,* published by Epiphany Press of Arkansas.

A strange melancholy pervades me
to which I hesitate to give
the grave and beautiful
name of sorrow

—Francois Sagan

This book is dedicated to my mother

Josephine Robertson

1915—1972

TABLE OF CONTENTS

Aunt Edith

Aunt Edith lived at the end of the streetcar line in Minneapolis
and every hour on the hour a streetcar would arrive
and the driver would snap out his black cashbox and swing down
to sit on the lawn for a smoke. More often than not,
Aunt Edith would join him and bring out some lemonade.

After having his smoke, the driver would turn on the electricity
and make sparks flash all along the overhead wires.
Then he would back up his streetcar in a long complicated maneuver.
and head back down to the Loop again.
My sister and I, fatherless girls, liked to visit Aunt Edith, and

since all of the men we knew were either dead, alcoholic or
streetcar drivers, we decided that we would live in a house like that
where men arrived pulling little electric stars all along the tracks toward you.
A place where men laughed out of the corner of their mouths,
and made you feel beautiful with the look in their eyes.

Oh, we knew that the men would disappear the way our father had,
so when they did, we wanted to be like Edith
and have a little stock of cigarettes and a bottle of sherry
so we could just go back inside and read another book.

Fatherless Woman

As a child, unfathered,
I inhabited a soft, woman's world of
Eau de Cologne and talcum powder.
I never swung from powerful hands,
knew of curses, beer, and pissing
never cowered in fear of a man,
or felt the scratch of whiskered kissing.

And all those years have left me this;
a weak joy at the sight of rolled shirtsleeves;
buttons undone at a man's throat.
A horse darkening the corner of a stable;
the smell of leather.

A legacy of waiting.

And now, undone, I find I love them all.
Indiscriminately, on street corners
smelling of Brut and Old Spice.
Enticed by the back of a man's head on a bus,
charmed by another's dark seriousness.

And I have stranger dreams of men unkempt,
uncivilized, primeval and unshaven.
All dead fathers, they are raging.
Oh, I know I am craven, craven.

Continental Drift

Now we discover that
the continents are constantly
moving and shifting

as restlessly as women
who are always arranging
and rearranging their rooms.

Beneath the ocean, giant plates
are continually grinding
against one another.

I imagine the great, deep
creaking and groaning, the
huge, sepulchral sighs

of Africa longing for America,
of Italy for the thighs
of an old mesalliance,

of the deep murmur
of the California mountains
still longing for their lost horizons.

At night, we shift in our sleep,
drift earthward, still searching
for a new realignment

while small earthquakes shudder
in a paralyzing parallax
and welter new mountains.

They bloom like insights.
We are beyond hope in this oceanic,
murderous plot to disconnect us.

O Kyrie Eleison (O curious liasons)
of continents and men.
Lie down with me, my only love

there is a whole ocean between us.

Love

Ah yes, I was there once
during the hurricane season.
A third world country, very little industry.
Chaotic, violent, but full of lush, fragrant
Mimosa and Cereus.

I remember the islands, I saw them at night,
the stars pulsating like amorous fireflies.
Of course, after the conquistadores left
everything ravaged, the city was in ruins.

I try to go back to it every now and then
but you know how it is
You pack your bags, you open your guidebooks.
You leave in the moonlight.

But this time you are older, wiser.
This time, you carry a handgun.
You kill anything that moves.

Lobster

On first seeing it, I was repelled
by the idea of eating something so
exotic looking and sinister,

having read Jean Paul Sartre's line
about crustaceans having a dubious
consciousness. But I was new in New York, and

the young man I had met there tucked
my napkin under my chin and
handed me a nutcracker for the shell.

I was from Minnesota, raised on
lakes and brook trout. I, too, was
uncooked and formless, like the creatures

who take on the shape of their environment.
My first taste was delicious, but the
third was even better and by

that time I was a real New York girl
who wore skinny black dresses and false eyelashes,
able to handle myself with any

crustacean, dubious consciousness or not.

Professor of Apocalypse

Halfway through the semester we
began to read the prophets.
Disaster was imminent for Israel;
they had broken the covenant.

"All flesh is grass;" you clearly loved
Isaiah and his poetry
and yearned for some apocalypse.
You told me you must change your life

and I began to imagine you in my future,
thought you might be
the closest thing to salvation yet

then I read the words:
"By the waters of Babylon I sat down and wept"
and I saw you one night in a dream
dragging your heavy Bible

full of lessons from history
and disasters you could count on.

Adding Some Words to My Mother's Gravestone

"Well I don't know," said the gravestone
carver at Mt. Hope Cemetery in Ashland, Wisconsin.
"That'll cost you. Words don't
come cheap you know. And the original
sentiment is usually the best."

When the aged voice went off to find a pen,
I thought of the sad transactions of headstones,
the business of perpetual care.

Say that I loved life, my mother once
said to me. Write it on my gravestone.
How could I have forgotten this?

Say that she loved life and say
that all of her children danced in her light
Say anything but do not write
Here lies the body of.

Was this a failure of the imagination
or were these just the most expedient words?
Say that "men must endure their going hence
even as their coming hither"

Say that "life is a bridge, go over it
but do not install yourself on it." Say
what the poets and prophets say
but say it in a new way.

Always I remember her out in front
tying up morning glories with a string
outside our old apartment window

struggling along as a single mother,
longing for a life of more eloquence.
Say that she loved life, that simple sentiment

and that all of her children danced in her light.

Antigone

Remember the year I played Antigone
with the Brooklyn Heights Players and you
used to come down on the subway to pick me up
at midnight after rehearsals?

How young we were then and how we loved
the theatre, although you wanted to become
a painter. We saw the "Fantastics" seven times
and each time we cried and went back to my
apartment to sing the songs and drink some wine.

That was the last time in my life I
will ever play Antigone and now I wonder
if it was really Antigone I played or her sister,
Ismene, who always did as she was told.
Being young was so much like being
a major character in your own life

And being young was wanting to be
Antigone, to defy authority, to assert your own
independence. All young girls want to be Antigone.

You once asked me: what is it really about?
And I said: about believing in a higher law,
about being our brother's keeper, about
someone being buried alive.

But after a while, I gave up acting. All that
waiting in the wings to go on, trying to be
somebody I was not, always mouthing
other peoples' words. After a while, I

lost my enthusiasm for it.

At the Mall

The salesgirl in Cosmetics who,
winding up her watch and yawning,
smiles at me as I pass, then
turns to inspect herself in the glass.
Our relations to each other are oblique and casual

here in this mall designed by someone who
has yet to discover
that all of the artificial plants in the world
will not recover paradise.

In Saks Fifth Avenue, candles shaped
like gorgeous sculptures stand voluptuously
dripping great rivulets of wax. They give
so little light, are so extravagant.
They feed the soul, like poetry.

The women shoppers dolefully meander
along the aisles of Liberty silk scarves, the
surfeit of luxurious goods. They can have
anything they want now, it appears,
but what they want is something more than this:

to be cashiered, cashiered, cashiered.

Down in the Ladies Room, the women stand
before the bathroom stalls like penitents,
but once inside, they scrawl impertinences
on the wall. Wild, bitter words

of tyranny, of gall.

Amtrak Poem

A woman on the train rises, prepares to leave, takes her coat.
Everyone watches her, half tranquilized
by the rocking train, the fading light.

A light in the car goes on, a sign
that dusk is falling, a rush of air
signals the opening and closing of doors.
People get on and get off all the time;

The world is the same; only the scenes change.
The names of the towns fly past, but they
do not signify. Only the red and burning sky.
Year after year, the restlessness.

And wherever you go, you carry it with you.
Dusk is falling, a rush of air
signals the opening and closing of doors.
People are trying to find their places.

So if a woman should happen to rise,
should take her coat, decide to go
should suddenly leave her place in line,
who will know what she leaves behind?

Amaryllis

You will bloom,
in spite of all benign neglect, all
screened-in rooms. Out here on the porch,
your red petals bugle out as if to say
you will bloom
in spite of this rain-filled day, this gloom.
The birds having already quit the feeder,
having lost their taste for sunflower seeds,
the lawn having already turned to yellow
and it's only June.
Coming upon you, I find your bright flower
balancing on that thick green stem with all
the insouciance of young girls
who insist upon mattering.

Emily Dickinson had that insouciance, too,
and she, too, insisted upon mattering,
although one critic called her "that little
home-keeping person;" although she, too,
was late flowering

and hid herself like you
for such a long, long time.

Poem for Midlife

Along the way, I began to see
that life was a journey

toward insight; became nocturnal,
grew to love the night.

Pulled out all the hairpins of regret
and let

my life fall free.
Along the way, I began to prefer

the description of a forest
to a forest.

Began to see that people die
for reasons other than old age.

Saw that my belief was a dead star
I could still get light from

And just when I thought there were
no more surprises for me

found poetry.

"If you don't trust sentimentality
you're not even in the ballpark."

—Richard Hugo

Kale Soup

The kale soup was delicious. She
had left it there in the pot for him
and gone out to do her chores and he
had eaten the soup and was happy with the taste.
His wife was out driving around somewhere
and he was leading the life he should
living in Cambridge among kindred souls
in a house that was very small and old.
He watched a squirrel on a feeder
taking what was meant for the birds.
So much was for the birds, really,
and what was it all about but this:
kale soup, his wife gone from the house
and this one afternoon of silence.

Two Thousand And One

That was the year Americans began
to get sadder. Faces became blander,
smoother. Nobody seemed interested
in politics anymore, or how to change
the world and make it better.
A cure for cancer was announced
and then revoked and reconsidered.
We seemed to be standing still
as far as progress was concerned,
An inquiry was made into some
atrocities in Vietnam, thereby
opening up that old wound again.

I was driving to Stoneham every day
to teach poetry, past the Big Dig
and watching the new bridge go up.
The bridge was white and looked
in the early morning frost like a giant harp
with its two towers, its thick white strings.
I knew Boston would never be the same
after this construction, which was the
only good thing that seemed to be happening.

Every day the seventh graders' poems asked
Why are we here? What is our perpose?
Where have all the brids gone? We will never NO!
I didn't worry too much about the spelling.
I told them about the new bridge in Boston

said they were all here on earth to help others.
Why the others were here nobody knew.
Said they were here to make the world better
and to find the Good, the True and the Beautiful,
just as Wordsworth had done when he stood on
Westminster Bridge and saw the sleeping city
which he compared to a giant heart lying still.

They seemed interested, still, they asked
their plaintive questions. To ask, at twelve,

the meaning of life, seemed incredible to me
and I could hardly read the two hundred poems per week
that sat trembling on my desk
waiting to explode into my heart.

Note written to the parents of a middle school child

I'm writing to say that your child seems to be
adept at writing poetry
This is a rare gift and should be nurtured.
Turn off the radio and the television.
Play Beethoven in the morning and Mozart at
dusk, before bed.
Resist speaking to him in the tone
of busy common sense
and give him a place where he can be alone.
Let him stay outside in the summer grass
for one whole night alone
Let him watch the moon
rise and the sun
set, let him stay in bed until noon.
Do not speak of obligations or of
things that must be done.

The students in this school are all
starving for beauty and for silence.
You see it in their eyes.
Bent over beneath their heavy backpacks, they are
already burdened
but when they read their poems aloud, it is like
the voice of God speaking.

They long for the wind-in-the-chimney sounds of poetry
and they too, like Odysseus, want to eat the cattle of the sun.
Everything around them is fast becoming elevator music, so
let them believe that they are going to the moon.

Moths

First, the tiny larvae ceilinged in situ
proclaiming their kingdom above the living
room, the plush tuxedo chairs,

larvae which we hoovered up prodigiously, the
machine gasping and wheezing with the sad
ingestion of bodies into a dust bag. Then

the moths arrived, full grown, mothering
above our heads; diffident, soft, half out-
of-sight. One night, we felt them pummel

our skin and we knew we were in for it,
bought moth balls, prepared for a fight.
Grain moths from our Health Food store;

we have exchanged pesticide-laden foods
for the constant fluttering of wings in the room,
the sense of never being alone,

The feeling of something in the corner,
a tick on the edge of our consciousness, a
nagging half doubt that won't go away,

like the words half forming sentences and
yet not making sense upon the page.

The Painters

When they walked through the house,
the draperies came down with a sigh,
the furniture slid by,
and from the corner of my eye
I saw my life rearranged.

Their footsteps creaked on my ceiling,
their brushes slid across my walls
and the melancholy motion seemed
like the absent minded stroking of dogs.

With their dark eyes and their moving hands,
they located the soft wounds of the house.
Windows whimpered as they scraped and cleaned,
a small sigh rose from the rafters.

Young and strong, they seemed to bring
a new surface to everything.
The rooms, blossoming into color
stared at me with an arrogance now.

At night, the painters left
to eat spareribs with their fingers
and to sleep with their wives
while I slid into the old soft clothing of youth,
the old habits of self reproach and,
sorting through my life, began

The years we lived in Cambridge

first, in the apartment on the Charles River where
the sycamores shed their skins to reveal
a patched nakedness, a pied sensuality, then
high up on the sixth floor in a grand apartment
filled with English antiques and a grand piano.
But when we found the house we wanted to buy,
life became, suddenly, less than it was.

Then, too, walking through Harvard Square,
there were always young people everywhere
laughing and talking. One day, I pass a young woman,
her arms filled with books and feel a flash
of her face in the yearbook years from now.
Her smile freezes and I feel my life
paginating, paginating,

and I become a fragment of her past
since these school years are always a part
of someone's past, as are these sepia trees and grass,
these pupils dilating letting in light. This
wind-swept yard, this meagerness of grass.
Will she remember it as I do? Will she recall
a middle aged woman she happened to pass
on a narrow path lined with statues
taking up space in the land of the living?

Selling the House

Every day, the soft murmur of voices
moving through my rooms
disturbing the universe. The baskets of
dried grass on the rafters, star quilts asleep
on the upstairs beds. Invasion of privacy!

The hanging spider plant clings to my shoulder
as I pass. Strange footsteps on my cellar stairs.
A salutary storm of sobs as some young child
complains and weeps about moving again.

The blond realtor pirouettes into the room.
She will tell the strangers that this is an old house,
a house that has been loved, that we would
certainly stay but for the sound of our own
voices, but for the way the days slide away fast,
we might linger, finishing up the dishwashing
after the important dinner.

And I would stay if I were not
a woman with a For Sale sign for a heart,
a woman looking to spend her remaining years
grander, in a house with more chandeliers.

The Kids

When they left, they took everything
that was worth anything.
They stood in the driveway

with my childhood, my motherhood
in their hands
and all my plans

for the careful cultivation
of two perfect beings.
They walked away

and I wasn't even finished.
I wanted them to have a spiritual life,
wanted to present to them

all the beautiful arguments for
the existence of God,
wanted them to know the difference

between lust and love,
between pleasure and good.
I forgot to tell them that a lot of things

were more important than a little
money in the bank, although now
I can't remember what they are.

And now I see that Dr. Spock was wrong.
He said that you could never
love them too much.

We did, and we were maimed
by their nonchalance.
Each morning, they arose

"Teach me to care
and not to care."
—T. S. Eliot

33

as spontaneous as poems
and they were, like poems,
mystifying, exasperating, asking for bread.

And now they're gone.
What was it, I keep asking myself
that I wanted them to be?

and then I remember. More like me.

Snow

This might be snow today and lovely but
it is not the snow of childhood and can never be.
It may be many things; drifting, excitable
in love with the earth toward which it falls,
but it can never be the snow of Minnesota,

Today, the snow is falling in Cambridge.
It has been falling all day, filling up all
the empty parking spaces on Brown Street.
At dusk, the garbage trucks trundle sadly down
the snow-filled streets like elephants.

The men in double-knit caps cry: pull her up!
They toss the blue recycling bins about with
weary arms, vexed by all the detritus of the world
and by the intrusion of the heavy snow.

Suddenly, they are gone and in their wake,
a sense of a chastened, whitened world.
The snow falls silently until nightfall
and in the magic of the deepened dark,
you keep on writing your poems and some

are melting into nothingness and some
are sticking and holding on, reaching someone
making that small human contact and
then, in that world so full of endless dark,
the world becomes so white you think

that even you might leave a mark.

The Great Bird Books

The great bird books are a thing of the past.
Only Audubon himself could describe
in violent and sharp beaked images
the descent of an eagle upon a lawn
alive with fantail pigeons.

He was in Spain at the time
in the heat of the Mediterranean near
the golden sands of Tarragona,
the *aprica littoral,* where all night long,
there'd been a thunderstorm.

And what of Levaillant of the
Histoire Naturelle des Perroquets who
hunted the lion and the leopard
in a court suit of blue-boy silk and white gloves,
in order to show his respect for animals.

Now there are few bird books left to discover,
and birds themselves are becoming few.
Only in London you might uncover
that masterpiece of the taxidermist's art
and mirror of the mid-Victorian age

originally shown in a special building
in the Zoological gardens at the Great Exhibition
and now relegated, forlorn and rather moulting,
to the Museum of Science in South Kensington:

Gould's twenty-four glass cases of hummingbirds.

In the Berkshires

These mountains, weary backdrops
to a muslin sky, why
these mountains have been ravaged
by a glacier

That melting blue coldness,
and rounding off of angles

In the silence of some distant past,
inundation, violation, by that
incubus of ice

In the silence, broken only
by the sound of water seeping,
these mountains, when they're sleeping,
do they yearn, I wonder, for that sudden, freezing

touch of ice?

Arriving, startled, breathless at the top, I find,
these mountains make me feel that I have lived
in valleys all my life.

Universal Gravity

The universe is expanding and all of the
galaxies are slowly moving
away from each other like raisins in
a loaf of rising bread.

Our universe is shrinking. Friends
drift away or die. Perhaps the detachment from
what we love most has begun. Why even you and I
sometimes it seems the distance between
here and the farthest star is closer than
the distance between you and me.

We imagine that we are alone in the universe,
but we, in fact, can only be seen
in reference to what is around us.
Without the other, we have no velocity.

And yet, look up, the stars are overhead.
The weary comet eternally returns.
Things stay within their orbit, more or less.

Up close, your eyes still burn with love and desire.
Perhaps those vows we uttered long ago are
sacred still, some words prevail to keep us wed.
Some force, some universal gravity
exists within our own small sphere.
Why else this solemn levity to charm me,
this sorry look, this bowed head?

"I was really too far out in my life
and not waving but drowning."

— Stevie Smith

High Mass at St. Paul's

The walls of the church
soar with indignation.

The crowd, kneeling and breathing,
clamorous and kind.

The choir, rising to such pure heights.

The relief in knowing there is something
higher than one's self.

Today, the priest steps
onto the altar

and the choir begins—
the *Agnus Dei*

Qui Tollis Peccata Mundi
sings the priest

and a child in the front row
begins to cry.

The child's mother rises
to carry him out

but he sees the priest.
No, no, I want to see Jesus, he cries.

This is the way it often begins:
A man is taken to be a god

and we are all down on our knees,
all thundering down in sweet surprise

like an ancient tribe, half terrified.

Letters from Home

The Minnesota handwriting — my own
before the years spent in London, before
this English script — these letters from home
hook into me with their honesty.

You can't do that, a sister writes
and I know she's right but I do it anyway.
God what a phony New York has made of you
writes my brother, like Holden Caulfield.

These letters erupt through my life periodically
and all of my persiflage, flippant,
New York fast talk
is only a gloss on the primary text
that I can't seem to find anymore.

I'm from Minnesota, from the heartland
of the Middle West. And the part that is
the poet in me, the part that is the very best,
is the part of me that never left.

An Evening Without TV

We were in love with the idea
But could we do it?

Outside, the sky darkened,
We eyed each other

Waiting for a clue. Even the news
Was no longer new

All the old insurrections,
The killings, the lootings, left us cold.

We did not, as of old,
Arrange ourselves upon the sofa

Facing the tube.
Doubt flickered in your eyes

As it used to long ago.
You fingered the pages of a book,

Timeless relic of the past.
It was not on the schedule, no,

But this evening would be different,
This evening there was a moon,

So you and I in the darkened room,
Began to explore each other anew

While the television, unplugged
And unwanted, throbbed with anticipation,

Cried silently: It's Me. It's Me.
Your old pie. Daddyface.

Man in a million. Dreamer of dreams.

Holy Ghost

The congregation sang off key.
The priest was rambling.
The paint was peeling in the Sacristy.

A wayward pigeon, trapped in the church,
flew wildly around for a while and then
flew toward a stained glass window,

but it didn't look like reality.

The ushers yawned, the dollar bills
drifted lazily out of the collection baskets
and a child in the front row began to cry.

Suddenly, the pigeon flew down low,
swooping over the heads of the faithful
like the Holy Ghost descending at Pentecost

Everyone took it to be a sign,
Everyone wants so badly to believe.
You can survive anything if you know
that someone is looking out for you,

but the sky outside the stained glass window,
doesn't it look like home ?

Painting the Steeple

Down on Brattle Street, they are
        painting the steeple of the Church of the
                Latter Day Saints and everyone

stops to watch as two young men in blue jeans
        hover, spread eagled as they work,
                hanging on for dear life to the church

below, which sits smugly self confident, as though
        assured of a place in the future. Old
                head in the clouds, dreamer of dreams.

The laying on of the thick white paint, so
        deliciously creamy and smooth,
                is mesmerizing to all, so much

like Moore's "unconscious fastidiousness."
        One can almost see a new church emerging
            from the old, a new way

to believe in something other than ourselves,
        something like fastidiousness, or perfection
            or God, for aren't we all, really,

just latter day saints waiting for the chance
        to reach the sublime? Aren't we all
                standing here, eyes skyward, just

waiting to feel the mystery again, wanting
        to say the word "Lord?" Lord,
            give us a sign.

Fire Island

The summer of the Moon Shot we
gathered in a friend's house near the beach
to watch the Apollo landing on TV
while the moonlight rode the waves along the shore
and upstairs the children slept.

Suddenly, you stepped out onto the deck
to change your bathing suit. I watched you go and
hardly breathed, for you, unsheathed
were like Apollo, radiant beyond imagining.

How like the sun we were when young,
innocent, suntanned and beautiful.
Carrying our children down to the beach

like satchels of gold, casting our rays
about us as we walked
Odyssean and inviolate.

Oh, Moon, you were wiser then,
before the Moon Shot you were still
master of love and the beseeching tides

Old Man in the Moon and Mister Greencheese,
better than television any night.
Once, you were pagan in your arabesques

Clouds like incense drifted past. We needed
the silence of you as much as the
vast inscrutability.

RISD

Graduation day in Providence.
The parents arrive carrying long-stemmed roses,
the mothers wear spanking new silks.
My daughter in her cap and gown sails across the street
toward us carrying a huge canvas.
The painting luffs in the wind and she cries:
"Coming About."

Charting her course, she moves to Chinatown.
Lives above a crack house, wears men's clothing
so she won't be mugged. She knows the power of her art
but she is like someone holding a diamond
who doesn't know what to do with it She feels the pulse
of the city, knows how to use adversity.

All night long she paints, then,
picks at her food in the morning, looks out
at the men lying on the pavement. What can I
do to help her? What can I say? I am in the

background now, a voice over the telephone
offering only abstractions in
my graduation poem: Soyez Sage. Carpe Diem. Take Notes.

Driving to the Cape

playing Oldies but Goodies on the radio, we
trundle futura, happy to be here, happy to be
anywhere at our age, when suddenly an old song
UNCHAINED MELODY takes me back and I am
standing in the rain with a young boy and we are
drenched and saturated in the music, and not even
breathing.

Now, speeding toward the Cape where we will
eventually retire, each new song pulls us back into time
into the old high way of love of the past, before
irony, before the fear of sentimentality, before the
terrible aversion to the literal, back when American
music was hopeful and cheery or Forget your Troubles
C'mon get Happy.

And I know that you, too, miss that old high
way of love, that almost religious experience
because when BLUE VELVET comes on, your eyes glaze
over and I know you're thinking of Francine Prendergast
and the Senior Prom at Englewood High in New Jersey
and I wish that I could get that same Old Feeling
too, but right now this is perfect; you just as you are,
you and I speeding futura into that small

spit of land called Cape Cod.

After 9/11

I used to love to watch airplanes
arriving and departing, climbing the sky.
So bold and full of bravura, as though
there were no such thing as gravity,

First, the plane on the tarmac,
the smiling faces at the windows
and then the great rush forward, the lifting off
as though momentum were everything.

The sheer insouciance of it, the machismo!
As though it was all
blue skies and fleecy white clouds ahead.
But clouds are not what they seem.

In order to fly you have to believe
that the pilot is God,
you have to become a child again,
small feet poised neatly under the seat.

Last week, another pilot took the wheel
and suddenly, all systems holding everyone aloft
were gone. Spinning toward oblivion,
did any have time to prepare themselves

when the one with fearful godlike powers
made the decision; the time has come?

Oh pray that they did not fear death so much
but felt, like Pascal, that moment of peace
when he "felt" God, that moment of certainty.
"Certitude, certitude, joix, paix," he cried to himself,

God of Christians and Jews,
God of Abraham, God of Isaac.
God of Abraham, God of Allah.

Gravity exists, said Newton, it explains,
the tides of the sea, the movement of planets,
the downward fall of heavenly bodies.

Nauset Beach

You see a wave like that, you wonder where it's been.
All around the world, perhaps. Maps cannot
contain it. Men have tried to describe it
but who can describe the sea's woe, the turbulence within?
Whitman once stood beside it crying "Camerado."
Santayana, the old philosopher, on its shore whispered:
"I do not believe you. God is great."

How quickly the land disappears on the Cape.
Every day more and more of this glacial deposit
being eaten away by the furious sea.
Soon, it will be the lost city of Atlantis.

Last year, the sea took away the life of a man I knew
in a boating disaster. What was the sea after?
He was a good man, a kind man, but he liked to say:
"Whenever I meet a man I like to think that I can take him."
The sea spews out dross, whatever is sand,
exhaling it all and then inhaling again
the whole ragtag bundle. Small stones, gulls' eggs
and all such stuff we carry home so lovingly
as if to say how inconsequential is our love of things.
As if to mock our essential cupidity.

Whatever the future was meant to be

it wasn't this. The night you went to the Cape cinema
          and the film was so violent you left early and
                    when you came out, the lobby was deserted.
                              All four theatres were playing to empty seats
                                        as though there had been a plague.

The wall-to-wall carpeting in the lobby was stained
          with Coca Cola and the walls were painted turquoise.
                    The popcorn popper was strangely silent in the
                              eerie glow of the dimmed lights; the giant
                                        Snickers and Milky Ways lay in a glass

tomb next to the biggest box of Raisinets you'd ever seen.
          Mountains of gum drops sat waiting in their long plastic
                    containers with scoops and bags at the ready. Outside,
                              in the parking lot, the air was cool. Stars were out
                                        and a few desolate people walked to their cars

eating boxes of candy. Across the road, lights flashed on the Dunkin
          Donuts sign and next to that, a House of Pancakes.
                    In the moonlight, the manager was spraying a
                              small patch of daisies near the theatre and as cars
                                        drove past, they gunned their engines.

And you wondered what happened to the world you once knew.

Bird Sanctuary

There is this other world
unimaginable, perhaps, until
you see the chickadee, how he cracks

sunflower seeds between his toes
and then pecks them open for the seed,
or hear the white-throated sparrow

singing of summer in a haunting song;
poor sam peabody, peabody, peabody.
The nuthatch descends the tree

head down, and the hairy downy wood-
pecker, named for his own physicality,
he too, sees the world differently.

Outside my window, three wild canaries
yellow with black wings
balance on the branch of a fir tree.

Long after they are gone
the branch continues to bounce,
heavy with their absence.

Look up! Now they careen
like a squadron of fighter planes
in an air show until

a blue jay rows in
like a police car on wings
frightening them away.

The air is full of flying things.
A sanctuary from the morning news.

Insomnia

Alone on the Cape in a new year
and all night long the thundering sea
invades our dreams, the stars anchor down
on these black nights like fate.

What can we do here but be ourselves?
The sea answers only to its own turbulence,
the moon rocks in its chamber,
the days flatten out into oblivion.

At night, you pace the living room awake,
the stifling cry of some night wandering loon
is company. I want to share your loneliness,
but loneliness cannot be shared.

I think of how I once had prayed
for a life of the finest intensity.
But what is poetry if not life
at its finest intensity?

The train

The train insists, with a furious hiss,
upon a slow start and then, gathering speed,
whispers with a sigh, becomes a slow
zipper closing the gap between city and country
between you and me.

And now it passes through Providence,
city of refuge and excoriation. How
providential to be here of all places, why
even the name Providence Cold Storage bespeaks
a heavenly place.

At Mystic, passengers board, tall,
mystical creatures with stars in their eyes.
Soon, the train's whistle wails with the plangency
of a failed trust, and then suddenly everyone begins
talking with everyone else, about the
failure of trains, the long delays. The unpredict-
ability! One can never depend upon them, that's
the beauty of it. How it unites us, this
failure of trains. We are all comrades now.

Then, suddenly, a loud laugh, like sudden glory
and shy eyes peer out and a child asks:
are we there yet? Are we there yet? He climbs
his mother like a mountain and her eyes glaze
over with happiness.

The conductor arrives, great weary wanderer
of the eastern seaboard. The children are crying:
Are we there yet? Are we there yet?
Trains cry in the night with the same plangent cry.

"The poet will tell us how it was with him
and all men will be richer in his fortune."

— R. W. Emerson

Coming Upon a Fragment of the
Gospel of Thomas in the Rare Books Library

What can I say to you
small brown fragment of papyrus?
You take my breath away, you

are still extant —
still live, breathe, in spite of all
the wet caves

the thousands of years.

The sadness of the Apocrypha!
Of all things pseudonymous;
all extra-canonical, not-quite-acceptable

writings they say
have nothing to say
but a great deal to add.

Latecomers to divinity
like Thomas the Gnostic who believed
self knowledge was the same as God.

Had this been Canon, we might have had
a gospel of Knowledge instead of Love.

Apocrypha: the hidden self
writing in obscurity
like so many who write poetry.

The fear of chaos invites taxonomy,
a listing of categories. Some writings
have to be left out of anthologies.

Some poetry, written by late-blooming poets
like me.

The Titanic

So this is how it feels, the deck tilting,
the world slipping away as one
sitting at a desk writes a check.

The Titanic went down titanically
like a goddess glittering,
Pinioned to an iceberg, she sank

almost thankfully while tiny mortals
leapt into the sea
and the band played Nearer My God to Thee.

But what happened to the signals of distress?
Nobody believed it was all really happening.
I still can't believe that it happened to me.

As a child, I stared horrified at the photograph
and the vision of that scene in the moonlit sea.
We will be one of the survivors, we think,
then something looms up like catastrophe.

All life, it seems, is the morning after
and love is the most beautiful of absolute disasters.

Flying Home from Rome

Suspended here above the land,
I love this chance at tempting fate.

The sense that I may never arrive.
The pilot in his Godlike voice

reminds us that we are passengers here.
We concentrate, like pagans, upon survival.

And when some dark barbaric clouds
invade our equilibrium, we

walk slowly down the aisles of the plane,
touching the seats lightly in benediction.

At the touching down, the blood runs red again.
Oh, we are angels at the terminal

and we smile at the embarking souls.

Class

In no time at all she began to see
that her students would have to read Plato,
that part in the Phaedo against suicide
for the world had changed so utterly

that they didn't know what to do with their lives
which they did not so much lead as follow
and for which they were overqualified.

She had not known there could be so many
casualities of modern life, but she
had read their themes and heard the cries
and so at night she sorted through poems.

She couldn't read Larkin or Eliot and the moderns
for they were cynics and so she gave
them Whitman to give a sense of self
and Hopkins "I'll not carrion comfort, despair,

not feast on thee."
then read to them from Emerson:
"Love your life, poor as it is.
Learn to endure solitude and neglect.
Above all, don't worry about being liked."

The Cafe Life

Out on the Cape, I saw the fox, lean and hungry
            trotting up the lane
and then I saw the little poodle from next door
            going out for his walk:
Some dark deed will happen, I fear.

My first job at Brady's drug store,
            I was fourteen years old
Mr. Brady was taken with my young mother,
            a young widow with four children

and every Christmas, he would bring
            a huge box of chocolates for us.
I remember biting into the nougats
            with some hesitancy

Welfare children, we were wary of luxury,
            distrustful of those bearing gifts.
But I remember the Whitman's Sampler with each
            chocolate labeled on the box cover

so that you always knew what you were getting.
            Each chocolate-covered caramel, every
coconut cream seemed to mean
            that someone might come like a wolf in the night

to keep the wolf from the door.
            But we were used to the life that we had.
We loved buying the cheapest Christmas tree
            and dragging it all together through the streets!

Liked wrapping our few meagre gifts
            in tissue paper from F.W. Woolworths,
                        liked having our mother all to ourselves.

Today, I have a cafe life and a Tiffany ring
            and sometimes I sit in the Paradiso Cafe
                        eating strawberry covered chocolate cake
                                    knowing I should be happy as a king

but I still don't trust it.

Ars Poetica

Who first felt fire, I wonder, who?
Who painted antelope at Alta Mira
who first discovered memory?
I must be he.

Who was the first to watch the trees
thicken with darkness as the sun began
to burn and extricate its light?

Who was the first to survive the night?
If I could just describe that sense, that sight,
I could be he.

Aunt Bobby

My favorite aunt was unmarried, half deaf
and lived alone in a smoke-filled room
at the Curtis Hotel in Minneapolis.
Once beautiful, she still had her vanity.

Her hip, mangled in surgery,
gave her a spasmodic gait, she flapped
down Oakland Avenue to visit us
like a tall crane who'd had a few.

I loved the sight of her, ran to
the frazzled, overpermed head, the
too-bright ruby lips, the strong perfume.
For all the appearances of inutile femininity,

she was to me, a half divinity.

The auntness of aunts, their
bemused, hat-askance objectivity.
They belong to no one and to everyone
and can offer a child another reality.

How many times she took me home
to her apartment hoping to give
my busy mother a small reprieve
handed me a pencil and drawing pad

then made me feel like Michaelangelo.
Now thinking back, I wish I had
given back just half of what she gave to me.

Animal Uncertainty

Spotted at the edge of a clearing, the doe
freezes and in that moment of hesitation,
carelessly exposes a brown flank
with all the insouciance of a woman undressing.

She lifts a delicate hoof and then
returns it to the snow with all the grace
of someone who was born to run. Once, long ago,
I watched an elephant near Madison square Garden

being coaxed onto a ramp. He carefully
placed his giant foot down, then stepped slowly back,
remembering, perhaps, a former collapse.
The elephant knows his great weight in the world,

how the earth opens up, sometimes without warning.
So much of our lives, we spend paralyzed
by indecision, or excessive ambition.
On good days, we go forward . . .

And sometimes, that elephant's look comes back,
that great moving mountain of animal sorrows
in moonlight in Manhattan. And the memory of that
midnight scene, that exquisite moment of

an elephant remembering.

The Poet

The poet is the lonely paperboy who
gets up early in the morning to fling out
his cares to the world.

In the early morning hours he rides
past the porches of sleeping people
who will stir, hear the small thud

of something falling against their hearts.
Most people, behind their walls,
see the sunset, feel the beauty of it,

have a sense of their own mortality
and yet do not know what to do about it
but in the silence of the night

when the moon rides into a cloud thigh
and a man whispers his love to a woman,
even the stars weep then.

When the dust forms on the earth,
when we shed our skin and hair,
when lactation in women begins,

therein, all poetry lies. The poet seeks
the dangerous places of the heart,
the white spaces of the page,

and so he starts each morning anew
to obliterate with words
the tone of busy common sense,

the terrible here and now.

Brown Dwarves

Newly discovered celestial bodies that contain
        planet-like weather with clouds of heavy metals
                and thunderstorms of liquid iron rain.

Fainter and cooler than other stars,
        they cannot withstand the necessary
                thermo-nuclear reactions and thus are called

Failed Stars.

And I, too,
want to live fainter and cooler,
        no longer want to be productive,
                have no wish for success and only want

to achieve the unattainable art
        of taking things just as they come. To
                stop and graze, to meditate, to

get on with my life sans regret, sans peur.
        My life with you.

And I sense in you as I sense in myself
        a world encompassing small rewards,
                a life of opportunities missed

and of situations unexplored.
        A life not really lived at first hand
                because of all of the books. Oh Lord!

How I carry that with me like contraband.

The Chain Letter

I would answer it if I could,
if I believed in providence, et al,
for I, too, know the consequences of
breaking the chain. I, too, feel the need
to connect, to manifest myself in words.

Dear Reader, it began, do not be afraid.
Great men and women have died for this
or for as much. Take the name from the bottom
and replace it with your own.

But could I do it? And so I began.
From Whitman, I learned the indolent capacity.
From Stevens, to resist the intelligence.
From Keats, to avoid the voice of
busy common sense.
Then, sitting alone, something pulled me
back by the hair. It was Emily, on the
art of sitting still. She had much to teach me, but

I learned more from one who didn't always
follow her own advice. Live or die,
wrote Anne Sexton. But don't poison everything.

Moving the Graveyard

Here and there, a few fresh graves
had just begun to settle in
and we had a difficult time of it.

So much deeper than we had thought,
something held fast beneath the rot.
I'd have left it alone if I could

but we had a job and it had to be done.
The headstones held like wisdom teeth
and we struggled with them, tried to read

the old articulations of grief.
Some stones cracked and then things ceased
to make much sense. "Until Christ comes

you will (will not) be saved."
Words by which one no longer lived.
And people passing tried to give

advice, some raised a hue and cry
about the sanctity of the dead.
And there were terrible gaps we'd made

with nothing yet to fill them in.
But we were just a bunch of guys
trying to do an honest day's work.

Yet I have trouble when I'm alone
sleeping at night when I think of it.
Wishing we'd let the poets lie.

"Changing the core curriculum
is like moving the graveyard."
— Derek Bok

68

"He who knows how to be poor knows everything."

—Michelet

The Wildest Word

The Benedictines had it, they knew
        the joys of silence, the illuminating of
                manuscripts, the careful diffusion of
                        esoteria.

The pleasures of abstinence.

Get to a point where you can deny yourself anything
        and then you are halfway there, some say.
                And poems are made
                        of love not made.

Emily Dickinson refused
        the offered touch and reveled in her own
                self abnegation. "The wildest word
                        consigned to man is No," she wrote.

"You love me best when I refuse."

        "Imagined love is better than the real,
                and occupies the highest branch of Eden's tree,"
                        wrote Edna St. Vincent Millay.

"Like fallen fruit, lived love is cheap."

Housesitting in Manhattan

In exchange for the care of a cat and a tortoise
        someone has lent me a brownstone in Manhattan.
                Each day I place the tortoise like a rock
                        into the garden for a daily walk.

I admire his passion, his ferocity
        when seizing upon a lettuce leaf, I
                see that all slow moving things prevail.
                        The ginger cat, a rehab from the rescue league

has been the victim of some sordid life it seems.
        Each day I feel her tiny claw marks burn.
                One day, the cat relents, and slides against me
                        and I soften and swoon.

Each day I sit with my creatures in the sun
        feeling the creatureliness of life return
                wondering, should I come back to live here
                        or is this now the city of the young?

And what does it matter where I live
        since I have all the requisite armor, the hard shell,
                the hidden claw, the heavy
                        animal sorrows.

Mea Culpa

The Bay of Naples is the sea of tranquility,
a longing for the sublime made visible.

In silence beneath fleecy white clouds,
two white tour boats traverse the Bay

streaming toward the beseeching shore,
trailing white lines behind them.

I stand, transfixed upon the terrace
of an old hotel, believing only

in the magnificence of this day,
while in the town of Sorrento, a vulgar display

of buying and selling beckons the tourist.
Today, the Pope has apologized for the sins

of the Church and its community.,
and the Bishop of Rome has compared the church

to Noah's Ark. "You could not have borne
the stench within," he said,

"if not for the storm outside."

In Sorrento, the church bells toll,
and we dress in white and head for church

The priest reads from Isaiah:

Remember not the things of the past,
the things of long ago, consider not.
See! I am doing something new!

Girl Scout Picnic, 1954

The parade began and the Bryant Jr. High School band
        marched through the streets of Minneapolis
wearing white shirts, blue trousers, playing John Philip Sousa

Lance, Jack, Sharon and myself on drums,
        strapped to our knees so we could play,
arms akimbo, drumsticks held high,

drum rolls, paradiddles, rim shots, flams
        while the trumpets groaned and the bystanders
cheered us on in the rain-drenched streets.

The Girl Scouts strutted ahead of us wearing
        their green uniforms, berets and badges
waving the Girl Scout flag, and smiling,

We could do anything after this, we felt,
        twirling our drumsticks between our fingers
Such joy seems unimaginable until I conjure it

Not even Wordsworth's memory of
        a field of daffodils comes close to it
The picnic later at the Minnehaha Falls Park,

then walking home much later in the dark
        still filled with the sounds of it.
To march at thirteen through the streets of Minneapolis

is to ride in triumph through Persepolis.

The Neighbor

Drink in hand, the neighbor tells me what a nice party this is and I see that he is not looking at me but at my piano. It's a little Victorian piece with built-in brass candlesticks that I brought over on the *SS France* from London after living there; an upright in a beautiful mahogany case.

The neighbor talks to me but it soon becomes obvious that he is dying to play the piano.

His fingers drum against his upper leg as he talks to the other guests, and then, when he does approach the piano he touches the yellowing ivory keys with reverence and the little piano once again feels the old association of elephant tusk and human desire. He opens the top lid to discover the bird cage action and then sits down to play as though there were nobody else around. He plays softly, turning his bent head into the room as people begin to enter and then he eases into the nocturnes, a little more loudly. He is a man who pianoizes every event in our neighborhood and everyone forgives him because he took up the piano late in his life and the rest of us are late bloomers too. It is only when he leaves the piano and visits the food table that I notice the candles on the piano are burning more fiercely as if to attract his attention once more and when he leaves, the little piano looks disconsolate, and I walk over to where it is smiling with its yellow teeth and I close the cover very carefully.

The Stroke

I ask my friend one simple question
and she flies into a rage. God? she cries
from her wheelchair. What has God ever done for me?

Now, paralyzed, she is all eyes. It is as though
something has forced her to a halt, ordered her
to sit quietly with her hands in her lap and do nothing.

Now, she can hear the clock ticking,
can almost hear, she tells me, the flowers growing.
I tell her about the students who lined up outside

Nabokov's class on Jane Austen, wanting to read
of a life where you did not have to Do,
just Be. The silence in the room is deafening.

I open the box with the strawberry tart.
When I hold the fork toward her, she
opens her mouth hungrily.
I notice that she eats two whole pieces.
Her mouth is stained with strawberries, she
will not be taken easily.

Diagnosis

All life expands to meet this
possibility. Some say
this is a natural process.
The body decays.
And why should anything last?

Someone reading your cast-
off journals in a flea market stall
might wonder at the urge to record
the names of birds, the rise and fall
of a conversation.

My friend, diagnosed
with Stage IV cancer, feared most
not death itself but the thought
he had not lived. His Roman face was always
wreathed in smoke and when he spoke,
it billowed out. He was too young
to lose his hair, his beard, his lung.
Soon, forced to his bed, he took to reading
Mary Baker Eddy

refusing to believe
that something as elemental as death,
something as full of beauty and distress
could ever be caused by cigarettes.

Memorial Service

Some speakers wept, recalling old ties
to the deceased, some were wildly
effusive in their praise
and talked of the dead man who had spent his life
travelling between New York and Boston.

The widow, her eyes rimmed with grief,
apprised us of our own mortality. No one
is surprised by death anymore.

It was untimely, though, he was only 51
and carried the disease in his family.
He must have been ready for what was to come
and yet two days before he died
the minister at his side asked

what's the plan?

The plan? The plan? The dying man
wondered aloud. The plan is to hold on
for a day or two and hope for a miracle.
Two days later, the miracle arrived.

Helen in Chemotherapy

"About being bald," she says,
advancing toward me in her wig
holding out her hands,

her small body, taut,
while the dance goes on,
the cells pirouette.

About being bald, she says,
delicately turning in the light,
"It's temporary, like cancer."
All day long, she whispers to herself
that the poison is not toxic but
a white, healing stream of grace

that will cure her, will release her
from this thing, this force
that is pulling her off center,

causing her imbalance.
In the center of the earth, someone is saying:

the Living have one more than
the Dead. At night, she hears the
argument, feels the earth

tilt on its axis. An imbalance,
yes, but she is strong. She pulls
herself upright each morning.

A Woman Diagnosed with Stage IV Ovarian Cancer
Decides to read all of Henry James

Because she, too, wanted
that kind of interiority. She, too
wanted to find a moral law.

She already knew that life,
like his sentences, was full
of qualifiers

and she, too, had a lively
aversion to the literal
and she wanted to believe

as he did, that death was
not ordinary but was, really,
the Distinguished Thing.

She felt like Strethers
in *The Ambassadors* who cried; "Live,
live while you can."

or like the man in the short story
who waited all his life for something
"rare and strange, that

sooner or later would overwhelm him."
I saw her near the end again,

in the lobby of the Oncology ward
always with a book in her hand, always
paginating, paginating, transmuting,

her life, perhaps, into something
as meaningful as fiction.

Wilting

After five days, our Easter tulips
      began to wilt, their bright green stems
            lengthened and reached out yearning toward the
                  light, their petals, as soft and translucent as human skin

dropped one by one and then
      their large white heads rested on the
            trestle table like tired children, like something
                  almost human

and we could not bear to throw them away,

Jane Austen died of Addison's disease, a
      failure of the adrenals, a gentle, creeping illness
            that begins with languor, lack of appetite
                  and a disinclination toward mental or physical effort.

The skin begins to look dirty, the mouth blotches,
      the body wastes and the patient gradually expires.
            Her mother "kept the couch" while Jane's bed
                  was fashioned from three chairs,

but for how long did she continue to write,
      her head drooping, each book reaching out toward
            the light, each one teaching us that if we are good,
                  we will be happy.

How much we need to be told this again and again.
      We already know how to die—what we want
            and need to know is how to live and
                  the pale lucidity of her words, those petals,

drop into the well of our experience like something
      almost human.

Emerson and Margaret Fuller

Unacquainted with adultery, the elephant
mates every two years and then
disappears for five days to return
on the sixth to wash off
the excess of love in the river.

Ralph Waldo Emerson admired his neighbor
Margaret Fuller and celebrated her
"approximate ubiquity" but
calling himself a "man of snow"
lamented his "porcine impossibility
of contact." And anyway, she knew
that he was already married,

though barely more than a
bachelor to his wife.

She has the "presence of a rather Mountainous Me"
he wrote in his journal. He noted her plainness,
her trick of incessantly opening and shutting her eyelids,
the nasal tone of her voice. All repelled him and he said
to himself: "We shall never get far."

"Let us leave off
this groping and touching" he wrote to her,
and so, although Emerson spoke
for whatever was wild and free, he
was not so free with Margaret who
wrote: "The Life. The Life.
When will it be sweet?"

"The poet cannot lie. He nothing affirms,
therefore never lyeth."

— Sydney

Henry James

"Poor Mr. James," Virginia Woolf once said:
"He never quite met the right people."
Poor James. He never quite met the
children of light and so he had to invent them.
Then, when people said: No one is like that.
Your books are not reality, he replied:

So much the worse for reality.

He described himself as "slow to conclude,
orotund, a slow-moving creature, circling his rooms
slowly masticating his food."

Once, when a nephew asked his advice
on how to live, he searched his mind.
Number One, be kind, he said.
Number Two, be kind and
Number Three, be kind.

At the Keats House

Keats, while dying,
whispered to his friend, Severn,
"Don't be afraid"— as if the living
were the ones needing comforting.

Below him, on the Spanish Steps,
the Bernini Fountain splashed playfully.
Crowds of people milled about,
arranged their packs, weary, perhaps

of Eternal Rome. A tourist,
fiddling with his maps, yearned for home
unaware that beside the stair
a posthumous life was beginning.

Now, we visit the house of the poet Keats
who died, some say, of bad reviews,
who lay with his treasure in these rooms
like Tutankahmun in his tomb.

Newton

Because of you, we understand the tides of the sea,
the movements of planets, the slow, remorseful
return of the comets. You are the mystery.

Alone in your room, in the park,
measuring the small degree of arc, sans love,
sans human conversation, loving only the
elegant equation

while outside, the apple-moon
falls toward earth and its embrace and the earth
gathers it in a swoon of soft and ever-circling
desire

Can one find happiness in the absence of
hypothesis? Love is the only thing that moves
the sun and the stars and the universe. This
is something we cannot prove. This
is pure hypothesis.

"I do not make hypotheses"
—Sir Isaac Newton

The Wife

It was not easy being
        the wife of poet Wallace Stevens, especially when
                the poet had a phantom lover
                        or what he called "the interior paramour."

Adultery in all but the physical sense
        it was a metaphysical love, the imagination
                working overtime in a man
                        bereft.

His unhappiness was boundless,
        but like many poets, he knew how to use it.
                Six foot three and two hundred pounds,
                        he was a vessel for poetry.

And what poetry! A world of blue guitars
        centaurs and imaginary gardens. And his
                blonde, well, his blond Elsie had hair
                        "like cow's spittle."

"I like Mr. Stevens poems when they are not
        affected," said Elsie Stevens. "But so often,
                they are affected." Elsie herself
                        was the model for the Liberty dime.

It was not easy being
        known as the woman with her face on the
                Liberty dime, while outside in the garden
                        her husband, fiddling with words on a page

reached the sublime.

London

Flowers flirting from window boxes.
Narrow, single-file streets.

Racing, furious clouds
like great wads of damp laundry.

The constant rain, weeping, weeping,
touching your face, sorrowing.

The shiny wetness of small streets,
like clean, well-licked spoons.

The tiny round cornered walls
To make you feel enormous.

Careless English gardens, rooms
of Chippendale and Turner prints

Small, measured glances in a crowd,
The small click of gates opening up.

Seriousness. A sense of conviction.
A need to hold to the difficult.

The possibility of conversation
as a way of life.

The possibility of a charmed life,
lonely and studious in a foreign land.

Venice I

Lungs bursting, heart aching, you
surface in Venice
dragging your indestructible luggage, your
unreadable guidebooks.

Sightseeing is a soporific and so
you refuse the daily hotel tour
to read in Ruskin that this is the
point of pause

where all of the opposite eddies of life
come together in rank water
charged with the fragments of the Roman Empire.

You scan the Piazza like a horizon,
enter the orient of St. Mark's Church.
Everything here contraband from Constantinople,
everything rising from the ashes of what came before.

The fruitseller sets out his apples and pears
in the marketplace alongside the Grand Canal.
The palaces float in voluptuous ease.
You sit in a cafe and think of home

where the light is hard and clear and bright
and you think that one more night alone
in a city of death, beauty and ashes
might be, at least for you, disastrous.

Venice II

When this city disappears
        into the sea like a crumbling cathedral,
           all memory
                will recreate a mythical Atlantis
                    or a bejeweled Troy

When this mysterious
        watery kingdom goes down
           then will this apprentice, this
                gondolier's boy in training for

his father's slow moving career
        of steering sedentary sightseeing souls
           through water that's been dead for years,
                will he cry "Oyeh" in his dreams

round darkened corners in canals of mist?
        Will we sit silently, all ears
           for the sound of a passing gondolier
                as we do now, imagining it?

Or will this beauty be dismissed
        as "cloud-capped towers, gorgeous palaces,"
           like Shakespeare's spirits melted into air.
                Will Venice fall, and will some witness

attempt to recall
        (safe on the mainland, far from the sea)
           that this was not Venice after all,
                but Dis, and this

the river of forgetfulness?

Florida

How can I tell you that I don't want to be here
when you have made all the arrangements?
I who love the sun as a brother,
relishing its warm basilica?

The women at the pool, offering themselves to the sun
How can they trust him, such a fickle one?
Nearby, it seems, you can swim with a manatee.

It's not that I'm unhappy here
It's just that every day the palm trees
strike defiant poses against the sky.

One day on a beach in Miami it comes to us:
we grow old and gravity pulls us south
and we grow heavy and thick with the years
going down.

Pull Over

The patrol car is behind me now with his siren going and red and blue lights flashing.

I pull to the side of the road and a young officer, all muscle and sinew, his hand on his holster, ambles over toward me trying desperately to look forbidding but he only manages to look like someone's little boy. His efforts to convey authority and to arrange his face to present a serious demeanor are betrayed by his dancing eyes and, once again, I am enchanted. He looks like a young father, someone who spends his evenings wrestling and rolling on the floor with his children.

I am to be admonished, it seems, vilified in front of a ragged band of onlookers attracted by the flashing red and blue lights who will ogle me as they once ogled puritan miscreants who ended up in the stocks. But what is it that I have done? Was it the U-turn that I made 30 miles back or something else? A vagrant fibre in me is exacerbated whenever I see a sign forbidding me to do something and anyway, even if I didn't do it, I imagine I did. I carry with me a free floating sense of guilt whether I've done something wrong or not and I am forever being pulled to the side of the road by someone who examines my credentials and says to me: husband, children, nice family. You want to go on for their sake, don't you? Then, do me a favor, pay the fine, keep it down to a slower pace. And then the truth between the lines, the knowledge that I have to face: Lady, you're not going anyplace.

To a Young Son

Today I passed your room
and you were slowly quietly
combing your hair.
It was a pleasant, calm moment.
I felt the silence of the room
and could almost hear you growing.
You combed without a mirror,
your eyes distant and pale,
your head slowly nodding
like the head of a stroked animal.

Xerxes the King sent out a spy
who returned to camp, astonished to say
that the Spartans were all stripped to the waist
their bodies gleaming in the Aegean sun
and they were all carefully combing their hair.
The king was afraid then.
The Spartans were preparing to die.

I turn slowly from your doorway
and return to the linen closet where I
will fold this memory in my heart
among everything that is clean and fresh and white.

The Death of a Dog

He was all climate and dogness and the odor
of the creaturely. He was Sam, the man in the dog suit
and Schneebrunzer, browner of snow.

The last day of him, in the
parking lot of the vet, tailgate open,
the doctor put him down
while a woman (me) sobbed unashamedly
and someone passing wondered aloud
at such emotion for a (mere) dog.

When was it ever such a comfort to grieve?
My sleeve carries the fur of him, my car
smells of him, my heart
breaks all over again
when I hear that bark in the moonlit dark
wanting to be let in again.

The Cat

All day, she moves through the rooms,
tail balancing above her, then
suddenly, she paws at the air:

invisible foe! She sits poised
for the washing down with
the merciless pink tongue.

Exhausted, she flops down
on the rug, stretches out and
arches her back erotically
aiming her serious look at me,

teaching me, once again
about longing, the terrible need
for touch.

But what does she suppose?
That I know nothing of voluptuousness?
That I have lost the feline,
indolent capacity, know nothing of

the whiskered kiss, the kneading
of the body, the soft circumference
of fur? The cloud of havoc and dander,
the mute face of desire?

Yard Sale

While I was spreading the old lace out in the sun
to whiten and dry, someone came by,
stopped to examine it
with careful and tentative hands.
Nobody knows just how long things will last.

While I was busily counting the coins
So much disappeared, gone into strange hands.
The black iron horses you had in a pair
and hated to sell, but put out in the end,

Someone came up to me simply to ask
how much I wanted for a pair of old chairs.
I would have given my whole life to know
just what was worth having and what was not.

I couldn't say, only sometimes at night,
I sat sultanic among my own things
As happy and smug as a king.

Neighbors arrived, began parking their cars,
walking all over the lawn. Some of them
hadn't been over for years. I watched as they stood
eyeing my past. There was my life

all spread out in the sun.
And what was the sum of it?
Dead poems that nobody would read,
the children grown and gone, no one to feed,

the dog's ashes still unburied.

Leaving Concord

When it was time to leave Concord, you said, I'm moving
    into the city. No more small town life for me, although, in fact
        it was the serenity of Concord that you loved, away
            from the fray

And then October would roll around
    and the trees would become a diorama of color
        and the leaves would pile up around your ankles
            making it difficult to walk away

and a few trees on Cambridge Turnpike
    were a brilliant yellow like golden lamps along
        the road and you drove beneath a canopy of fire and light
            and then you couldn't go.

And then the children would arrive in Halloween costumes
    and the smell of pumpkins and burning leaves along Lowell
        Road would keep you tethered to your place, the past
            breaking out in your heart and so you stayed

And then winter would arrive, the snow bandaging the fields
    whitening away the horizon. And then you'd take your skis
        into Estabrooks woods, your dog racing ahead, ruining the
            trail. Something would pile up against

the door making escape difficult and the house became a hushed
    cathedral and you would sit by the fire, eyes glazed,
        listening to the slow dropping of wet snow.
            At night the snowplows would arrive

with their midnight groanings and shovelings.
    Suddenly, in the moonlight, the road was visible.
        And so you said that now you'd go,
            But then spring came babbling in with crocuses and

daffodils and the Garden of Littles sprang to life and all the
    flowers came in waves then, first the whites and
        then the deep purple Siberian iris and then peonies, ribald
            red and then you said you'd go.

But then, waking in the morning, you could see
      the pond beyond your house covered by a quilt of fog,
            a pillow of mist, waiting for the morning to clear its
                  throat, waiting for the young gods to be kissed.

And you longed, then, to be like the fog, hovering above life,
      or like the pond, the marsh filling up all the empty spaces
            and suddenly it was summer.

And sometimes in August the house was so hot, you cursed
      the day you ever moved into it. Nature turned rank
            and you were deep in weeds and mosquitos.
                The humidity was unbearable, the garden had fought back

and won and summer felt like an unwanted visitor,
      a woman in a rump-sprung robe, smoking and drinking gin.
            The mood that you were in, you'd pray this guest
                of summer would not stay and then

just when you thought you'd leave, a wren
      built his nest above your porch among the eaves
            and hatched a nest of fledglings

But then one day, you did go, although somehow, you knew
      that you could never really leave Concord.
            It had become a part of what you were, a place
                where you had raised your children

a place untouched by time and space, a place to think of
      late at night, alone. There would always be this Concord,
            this Concord of the mind and no matter how many
                times you left it, it would always be home.

NOTES

The poem "Emerson and Margaret Fuller" takes quotes from Richardson's biography of Ralph Waldo Emerson and scatters them throughout the poem.

The poem "The Great Bird Books" is a found poem, using prose from a 19th century bird book and breaking it up into lines while inserting lines of my own. The last three stanzas are original lines.

"Adding some words to my mother's gravestone" includes quotes from *King Lear* and the sayings of Jesus.

In the poem "Leaving Concord" the line "guest of summer will not stay" is from Shakespeare.